Understanding the Eucharistic Prayer

Charles Read
Director of Licensed Lay Ministry Training,
Diocese of Norwich
Director of Liturgy, Eastern Region Ministry Course

GROVE BOOKS LIMITED
RIDLEY HALL RD CAMBRIDGE CB3 9HU

Contents

Preface

Several members of the Group for the Renewal of Worship thought we might make available the material we use in teaching ministry students about the Eucharistic Prayer. In the end the lot fell to me to produce a booklet and I am very grateful to other Group members who shared their teaching ideas with me and that includes most especially Phillip Tovey and Colin Buchanan who have mentored this booklet. I am also grateful to students at the Wesley Studies Centre and Cranmer Hall and more recently students at the Eastern Region Ministry Course who have been on the receiving end of much of what follows and thereby helped me to refine it. Biblical quotations are usually taken from the NRSV though occasionally I have made my own translation where I do not think the NRSV is clear enough (for my purposes!).

CW = the Church of England's *Common Worship* set of books
MWB = the British Methodist Church's *Methodist Worship Book*

First Impression November 2022
ISSN 0144-1728
ISBN 978 1 78827 275 9

1

The Naming of Parts

The central prayer at a service of Holy Communion goes by different names. These are some of the most common.

- *Anaphora*—the Greek name, and means 'lifting up' (and hence might imply offering).
- *Prayer of Consecration*—the *Book of Common Prayer* uses this term.
- *Eucharistic Prayer*—this title focuses on the prayer as an act of thanksgiving and is the most Biblical term.
- *Canon*—a Latin term referring to the Canon of the Mass, indicating that this prayer is the standard prayer (canon means 'rule' or 'measure').

A eucharistic prayer has several parts, though it is one prayer. The example below is the first Eucharistic Prayer (A) from *Common Worship*. Note that the order of the parts is not the same in every eucharistic prayer and it is important to grasp the differences. In the Church of England, as in the Methodist Church, the different shapes do not represent different theologies and each prayer is intended to be able to be used by the whole church.

The Lord be with you
and also with you.

The first two lines are **The Greeting**.

Lift up your hearts.
We lift them to the Lord.

Let us give thanks to the Lord our God.
It is right to give thanks and praise.

The next part of the opening dialogue is the ***sursum corda***—Latin for 'lift up [your] hearts.'

It is indeed right,
it is our duty and our joy,
at all times and in all places
to give you thanks and praise,
holy Father, heavenly King,
almighty and eternal God,
through Jesus Christ your Son our Lord.

The section from here to the Sanctus is called ***the preface***—there can often be variable texts to match the church year (seasonal prefaces) or a theme. These are called ***proper prefaces*** as they are appropriate ('proper') at certain times and in

For he is your living Word;
through him you have
created all things from the beginning,
and formed us in your own image.
Through him you have freed
us from the slavery of sin,
giving him to be born of a woman
and to die upon the cross;
you raised him from the dead
and exalted him to your right hand on high.
Through him you have sent upon us
your holy and life-giving Spirit,
and made us a people for your own possession.

certain situations. In some CW prayers you can write your own prefaces.[20] Proper prefaces can replace the whole preface or be shorter insertions at the end of the standard preface.

Therefore with angels and archangels,
and with all the company of heaven,
we proclaim your great and glorious name,
for ever praising you and saying:

Holy, holy, holy Lord,
God of power and might,
heaven and earth are full of your glory.
Hosanna in the highest.

This section is ***the sanctus*** (Latin for 'holy').

[Blessed is he who comes
in the name of the Lord.
Hosanna in the highest.]

This section is ***the benedictus*** (Latin again, meaning 'blessed'). The full title is *Benedictus qui venit* ('Blessed is the one who comes'). (On the reason for the brackets, see below.)

Accept our praises, heavenly Father,
through your Son our Saviour Jesus Christ,
and as we follow his example
and obey his command,
grant that by the power of your Holy Spirit
these gifts of bread and wine
may be to us his body and his blood;

A prayer for the Spirit is called an ***epiclesis*** (Greek this time, meaning 'call down'). See note at the end of this chapter on different types of epiclesis.

who, in the same night that he was betrayed,
took bread and gave you thanks;
he broke it and gave it to his disciples, saying:
Take, eat; this is my body which is given for you;
do this in remembrance of me.

Recalling the last supper is called ***the institution narrative.***

In the same way, after supper
he took the cup and gave you thanks;
he gave it to them, saying:
Drink this, all of you;
this is my blood of the new covenant,
which is shed for you and
for many for the forgiveness of sins.
Do this, as often as you drink it,
in remembrance of me.

Therefore, heavenly Father,
we remember his offering of himself
made once for all upon the cross;
we proclaim his mighty resurrection
and glorious ascension;
we look for the coming of your kingdom,
and with this bread and this cup
we make the memorial of
Christ your Son our Lord.

The act of remembering is called ***the anamnesis*** (Greek again). It picks up the remembrance from the Narrative of Institution.

Great is the mystery of faith:
Christ has died:
Christ is risen:
Christ will come again.

These ***acclamations*** are often called memorial, eucharistic or communion acclamations.

Accept through him, our great high priest,
this our sacrifice of thanks and praise,
and as we eat and drink these holy gifts
in the presence of your divine majesty,
renew us by your Spirit,
inspire us with your love
and unite us in the body of your Son,
Jesus Christ our Lord.
Through him, and with him, and in him,
in the unity of the Holy Spirit,
with all who stand before you in earth and heaven,
we worship you, Father almighty,
in songs of everlasting praise:

This prayer has another ***epiclesis*** here.

Blessing and honour and glory and power be yours for ever and ever.
Amen.

This section is the ***doxology*** (Greek *doxa* = glory). The Amen is often called ***the Great Amen***.

Here is another example, from the *Methodist Worship Book* (MWB).

The Lord be with you.
And also with you.

Lift up your hearts.
We lift them to the Lord.

Let us give thanks to the Lord our God.
It is right to give our thanks and praise.

The **greeting** and ***sursum corda*** as above. NB The MWB includes 'our' in the last line.

It is indeed right, always and everywhere,
to give thanks to you, the true and living God.
Endless is your mercy and eternal is your reign.
All creation rejoices in your radiant splendour.

You made a covenant with your people
and declared your purpose of justice and love.
When all things were ready,
you sent your Son to be our Saviour.
In words and deeds
he proclaimed your kingdom,
and obeyed your will even
to death on the cross.

Through his mighty resurrection
he overcame sin and death
to set the whole creation free.

Therefore with saints and angels
and with all the choirs of heaven,
we join in the song of eternal praise:

Preface, as above. The MWB has seasonal Eucharistic Prayers rather than the CW practice of inserting seasonal prefaces into the prayer, though there is provision for writing your own entire eucharistic prayer, which permission the Church of England does not give.[21]

Holy, holy, holy Lord,
God of power and might,
heaven and earth are full of your glory.
Hosanna in the highest.
Blessèd is he who comes in the name of the Lord. Hosanna in the highest.

Sanctus and **benedictus** as above, but note that there is nothing in brackets, unlike the CW practice—see note below.

We praise you, Father,
that on the night in which he was betrayed,
our Lord Jesus took bread and gave thanks,
broke it, and gave it to his disciples, saying,
'Take and eat. This is my body, given for you.

Institution narrative, as above.

Do this in remembrance of me.'

After supper, he took the cup, gave thanks,
and gave it for all to drink, saying,
'This cup is the new covenant of my blood,
shed for you and for all people
for the forgiveness of sin.
Do this in remembrance of me.'

As often as we eat this
bread and drink this cup
we proclaim the Lord's death
until he comes.

Acclamations—NB no options given, unlike CW.

Therefore, gracious God,
with this bread and this cup
we remember that our Lord
offered his life for us.

Anamnesis, as above.

Believing the witness of his resurrection and ascension, we look for his coming in glory, and our sharing in his great and promised feast.
Amen. Come, Lord Jesus.

This prayer has other congregational acclamations—as do some CW prayers.

Send now, we pray, your Holy Spirit,
that these gifts of bread and wine
may be for us the body and blood of Christ
and that we may live to your praise and glory
with all your saints in light.
Amen. Come, Holy Spirit.

The **epiclesis**—a mixture of consecration and communion epiclesis (see below).

Join our prayers
and the prayers of all your people
on earth and in heaven
with the intercession of Christ,
our great high priest,

through whom, with whom,
and in whom, in the unity
of the Holy Spirit,
all worship and honour are yours,
almighty God and Father,
for ever and ever. Amen.

Doxology

Prayer for the Spirit (epiclesis): There are broadly speaking two types of epiclesis. A *consecration epiclesis* asks the Spirit to do something to the bread and wine. (I discuss what exactly the Spirit is supposed to do in chapter four.) A *communion epiclesis* asks the Spirit to do something to the people who receive the bread and wine. Many eucharistic prayers have two epicleses—often one of each. In the example above, the first epiclesis is rather ambiguous—it begins by being a consecration epiclesis (asking the Spirit to make the bread and wine the body and blood of Christ) but is also a communion epiclesis (the bread and wine are to be the body and blood of Christ 'for us'). The second epiclesis in the CW example above is a clear communion epiclesis. In the epiclesis it is also important to note the verb. Here it is 'renew,' but more common generally is 'send' or 'come' (for example, 'Come Lord').

Benedictus: In CW, this is enclosed in brackets which indicates it is optional. This has been the practice in Church of England services since the 1960s and is there because some people are concerned that adding the Benedictus to the Sanctus implies the real presence of Christ in too literalistic a way—I discuss this more later in the booklet.

Where Do Eucharistic Prayers Come From—and Why Have Them? 2

From Last Supper to Eucharistic Prayer

The accounts of the Last Supper in the Bible just say that Jesus gave thanks over bread and wine. They do not tell us what he said. It is often assumed that he used a form of the Jewish prayer over meals called the *birkat hamazon*. We do not actually know whether this prayer existed at the time of Jesus and we are dependent on later Jewish evidence but the text of the later version of the prayer is:

> Blessed are you, Lord our God, King of the universe, for you nourish us and the whole world with goodness, grace, kindness and mercy. Blessed are you, Lord, for you nourish the universe,
>
> We give thanks to you, Lord our God, for you have given us for our inheritance a desirable land, good and wide, the covenant and the law, life and food. Blessed are you, Lord, for the land and for the food.
>
> Have mercy on us, Lord, for your people Israel, and your city Jerusalem, on your sanctuary and your dwelling place, on Zion, the habitation of your glory, and the great and holy house over which your name is invoked. Restore the kingdom of the house of David to its palace in our days, and speedily build Jerusalem. Blessed are you, Lord for you build Jerusalem. Amen.[1]

By the time we get to the middle of the third century, we are beginning to see eucharistic prayers like the ones you find in churches today. It is by no means clear how the eucharistic prayer developed in the very early stages but we get a clue in Justin Martyr who was writing in the middle of the second century. He refers to the person leading the service praying for as long as he is able.

Many scholars think that the very early eucharistic prayers were improvised by the bishop presiding.[2] These improvisations begin to take on a fixed form not least with the discussions of correct doctrine in the church. (When Christians were working out what exactly they believed about Jesus in the third and fourth centuries, it became important to write this down carefully, not least in prayers used frequently in worship.)

By the fourth century we are beginning to see actual eucharistic prayers written down and preserved through history. The basic shape of these is very similar to the ones we are used to in the Church of England and the Methodist Church today. This is a shape which is found in Roman Catholic eucharistic prayers as well as in the Lutheran church and in many other denominations which have a fixed liturgy.

Why Have One Anyway?

Some modern Christian traditions do not use a eucharistic prayer as such but simply read a biblical text (often 1 Cor 11.23–26) followed by the sharing of bread and wine. There are other churches which read a text such as 1 Cor 11 then have a short prayer of thanksgiving which does not include the institution narrative. These approaches, where the reading of the 1 Corinthians text functions as a mandate for sharing communion, are relatively recent and most churches will use some form of eucharistic prayer.

There are essentially two reasons for doing this.

- Historically, having a eucharistic prayer is what Christians have done going back to the earliest times for which we have clear evidence (the third century). Not having one is the exception not the norm.
- Theologically, what we are doing at Holy Communion is giving thanks. To do this you need a prayer of thanksgiving of some sort. Just reading a part of 1 Corinthians does not do the job, though this biblical text has almost always been a key component in a eucharistic prayer.

3

Structures

To understand the theology and meaning of an act of worship, it is often helpful to look at the structure. Different sorts of structures can be discerned in the same act of worship and when it comes to Holy Communion there have been at least three ways of understanding the structure.

Gathering/Word/Meal/Dismissal

This understanding of the service has been popularized by a variety of North American writers such as Gordon Lathrop.[3] It is a very basic structure which sees a communion service as being an act of worship of two parts (word and meal) with gathering and dismissal sections added. A World Council of Churches consultation in 1994 noted this pattern (often called an *ordo*) in its report—called the Ditchingham Report as the consultation met at what became the Belsey Bridge conference centre in Ditchingham, Norfolk. It commented:

> This *ordo*, which is always marked by pairing and by mutually re-interpretive juxtapositions, roots in word and sacrament held together. It is Scripture readings and preaching together, yielding intercessions; and, with these, it is eucharistia and eating and drinking together, yielding a collection for the poor and mission in the world.[4]

Note that word and prayer are linked here, as are thanksgiving and mission.

Word and Sacrament

An older way of interpreting the structure is just to talk about the service being about word and sacrament. There has long been a sense within Protestant and especially evangelical circles that these two elements need to be held side by side as equally valuable and important components. This can be seen in the theology of John and Charles Wesley and others in the early evangelical revival in the eighteenth century. Later evangelicalism tended to value word more than sacrament and there was an attempt to go back to the original balance between the two in statements from the first two National Evangelical Anglican consultations at Keele in 1967 and Nottingham in 1977. It is debatable whether this attempt at rebalancing so that communion is again valued more highly has so far succeeded in contemporary evangelical Anglicanism.

Four-action Shape and its Revisions (Two-action Shape)

The most famous and possibly most important shape was discerned by the Anglican scholar Gregory Dix and published in his huge and hugely influential book *The Shape of the Liturgy.*[5] Dix discerned that in the New Testament there was a seven-action shape to the communion service. This was because communion was held in the context of a real meal and so the different actions taking place within the communion part of the service were interspersed with courses of the meal. Thus you get:

- Taking of bread
- Giving thanks over bread
- Breaking bread
- Sharing bread
- Taking wine
- Giving thanks over wine
- Sharing wine

All of these had courses of the meal in between them. When the meal stopped happening (perhaps because of the abuse taking place in places like Corinth where the rich ate their fill and the poor coming later got the remainder or even inferior food), the 7 actions could be combined so that you dealt with the bread and wine together. Thus you get four actions which Dix alleged was the ancient structure of the communion part of the service:

- Taking bread and wine
- Giving thanks over bread and wine
- Breaking the bread
- Sharing bread and wine

This is the four-action shape for which Gregory Dix is famous. It is not particularly controversial at this stage of his argument since you can see these four actions in ancient communion services. He went on to say that these four actions evolved into parts of the service which carried particular theological ideas. So here

- Taking bread and wine became the offertory
- Giving thanks over bread and wine became the eucharistic prayer
- Breaking the bread became the fraction
- Sharing bread and wine became communion

This is where many subsequent writers part company with Gregory Dix as his theory of historical development is too neat—real acts of worship evolve in a rather untidy way. There is particular controversy over the idea of offertory (that is, the offering the bread and wine to God).

However, the basic four-action shape has won the day and modern communion services use it as their basis. It was particularly strong in the *Methodist Service Book* (1975) and the Church of England's *Alternative Service Book* (1980).[6] It is important for services to make this shape clear and that is why in modern services we do not break the bread in the middle of the eucharistic prayer, as happens in the *Book of Common Prayer* service which uses a different shape. Indeed, Dix thought the BCP shape was an aberration in the history of the communion service.

There has been a significant revision to Dix's shape in that some more recent writers see the two important actions as being giving thanks over the bread and wine and sharing bread and wine. The other two actions of taking and breaking then become functional: you take in order to give thanks and you break in order to share.[7]

Structures for the Eucharistic Prayer

You will see from chapter one that many modern eucharistic prayers follow a trinitarian structure. This is also true, in the main, of eucharistic prayers throughout history. So after the opening dialogue (*sursum corda*), there is a section focusing on what God the Father has done. This is the focus of the preface and may also move into giving thanks for what Jesus or the Spirit or even some human beings have done but it is in the context of giving thanks to the Father.

The focus shifts to Jesus the Son in the middle of the eucharistic prayer around the institution narrative. Towards the end, the focus shifts again to centre on the work of the Spirit. The prayer normally concludes with the doxology and what is known as the Great Amen though in *Common Worship* Eucharistic Prayer H moves the Sanctus to the end to form a climax of praise.

Structure and Theology

One of the structural issues which connects with theology is where you put the epiclesis—and there might be more than one in a eucharistic prayer. If you think that the institution narrative is the most important part of the prayer (which we look at in the next chapter), then you might want to pray for the Spirit early in the prayer so the Spirit is ready and waiting to act when you get to the institution narrative.

Alternatively, if you think that the prayer for the Spirit is a more important part of the prayer then you might want to put that part of the prayer later on within the eucharistic prayer. As we will see later, modern ecumenical consensus has it that it is the whole prayer which consecrates the bread and wine so it is unhelpful—in fact quite wrong—to put emphasis on one part of the eucharistic prayer over and above the whole prayer.

4 Theology

Whether we like it or not, Holy Communion is a ritual, and the eucharistic prayer is a central part of that ritual. It may well be that we can understand the eucharistic prayer by looking at ritual theory. We need to be careful here because ritual theory is a very large field and covers a great number of human activities, not just worship. Nor is it the case that all ritual theorists agree with each other! Some broad insights might help us to understand what is happening in the eucharist and in the eucharistic prayer.

- *Expressing the inexpressible.* We all know those times when we cannot find the words to say what we are thinking. We also know the saying that a picture is worth a thousand words. Rituals can often help say something when words are inadequate. We can understand the sharing of bread and wine at Holy Communion as saying something about our relationship with God which we cannot fully put into words.

  However, the eucharistic prayer tries to do just this. That is why most eucharistic prayers use picture language to talk about what is happening. As texts, they are more like poems than doctrinal statements. (This does not mean that they do not contain doctrine—in fact the reason why the Church of England only allows the use of authorized eucharistic prayers is precisely because they are important vehicles of doctrine and therefore need to be regulated through the processes of General Synod and the House of Bishops.)

  What this insight does indicate, however, is that the eucharistic prayer alone is not enough if it is not accompanied by actual eating and drinking. This was a key part of the understanding of Thomas Cranmer and the whole question has resurfaced in recent years during the pandemic when practices such as spiritual communion and receiving communion in one kind became prevalent again. These practices raise big questions about whether this is an adequate way of engaging in Holy Communion.[8]

- *Building a relationship.* We build relationships with other people through engaging in shared rituals and meals. In this way, receiving communion together builds fellowship in the local congregation and in the church generally. The eucharistic prayer will therefore often make some reference to how this happens. This is frequently through a communion epiclesis, as discussed above. As well as this, in receiving communion we build our relationship with God.

- *Deepening our relationship with God.* People who study rituals often classify them in two different types depending on what the rituals are trying to help people do. So some rituals help us to navigate our way through changes in life such as bereavement and getting married. Ritual theorists have often identified rituals which they call rites of intensification which deepen an existing relationship.

  Holy Communion can be seen as one of these rites of intensification. Eucharistic prayers will almost always make reference to how we are growing in discipleship and getting closer to God. This is the major spiritual reason for having a eucharistic prayer.

These insights from ritual studies can help us to understand what is happening in Holy Communion and can help us to spot some of the themes of eucharistic prayers. However, much more can be said if we consider more overtly theological matters such as consecration, offering and thanksgiving.

Consecration—How it Happens

One of the key theological discussions around Holy Communion is to do with the idea of consecration. Colin Buchanan has helpfully clarified that there are two questions here which are separate but connected.[9] He describes this as what effects consecration and what does consecration effect. In other words, if you are (or rather God is!) going to consecrate bread and wine how do you do it and then when you have done it, what has happened?

Before we look at answers to these questions it is worth asking if they really are useful questions! Western theology (both Protestant and Catholic) has tended to focus on these questions but eastern theology has not been so obsessive about them—but even in the East such questions have needed to be addressed. They run the risk of focusing on what the presiding minister is doing whereas Eastern approaches are more concerned with what God is doing. Whatever consecration happens, it happens because of what God does. The minister is (only) voicing the prayer/desire of the congregation.

They have been three main ways of thinking about what consecrates the bread and wine.

- *Reciting the institution narrative.* This is the view that thinks the words of Jesus spoken at The Last Supper as recorded in the New Testament are what make the bread and wine into the body and blood of Jesus when the person presiding speaks these words over the bread and wine on the communion table. This view became the dominant one in the Western church in the Middle Ages and can be seen very precisely worked out in the theology of Thomas Aquinas (1225–1274) though it goes back to Ambrose in the fourth century. Geoffrey Cuming describes the precision as Aquinas describes it like this: 'The word "transubstantiation" was used by the Lateran Council of 1215; and sooner or later the question was bound to be asked "When does it happen?"[10]

  Thomas Aquinas laid it down that "the sole and essential form for the consecration of the bread" is the words *Hoc est corpus meum* [*This is my body*], and for the wine, from *Hic est calix* [*This is my blood*] down to *remissionem peccatorum* [*remission of sins*]. Even if the rest of the Canon were to be omitted, as long as these words were spoken, the elements would be consecrated. Transubstantiation takes place in each case in the last instant of the words being spoken. Thus the consecration of the bread is completed before that of the wine is begun. The "moment of consecration" could scarcely be defined more stringently.'[11]

  This view looks for a very specific moment when the consecration happens. In some churches it is marked by bells being rung and by the consecrated bread or wine being held up by the presiding minister.

- *Praying for the Holy Spirit to consecrate the bread and wine.* This view has been more popular in the Eastern church and attaches great significance therefore to the (consecration) epiclesis within the eucharistic prayer.

- *The whole eucharistic prayer consecrates the bread and wine.* This may be described as the modern ecumenical consensus. There is no specific moment of consecration as there is in the previous two views. By the time you get to the end of the prayer, consecration has happened. This view fits with some contemporary charismatic and Pentecostal theology which sees praise as efficacious. When God's people praise God, something happens. In the earlier history of the charismatic movement there was even a book published called *Power in Praise.*[12]

- *Setting aside by prayer consecrates.* There is an older more Reformed view that by setting aside bread and wine through prayer, they have been permanently consecrated for holy use. 1 Timothy 4.4–5 which says, 'For everything created by God is good, and nothing is to be rejected, provided it is received with thanksgiving; for it is sanctified by God's word and by prayer,' is seen as the foundation of this view. It can accommodate a variety of approaches to 'What happens to the bread and wine?'

It is arguably the theology of the 1662 *Book of Common Prayer*, and explains the manual acts (taking of the elements in the Narrative of Institution) and the rubrics for consumption of the elements which have not been shared in receiving communion.

Consecration—What it is

The question here is not simply what happens to the bread and wine when the presiding minister prays over them, it is also a question of where Jesus may be found at a communion service. There are broadly speaking three ways in which Jesus is thought to be present at communion:

- In the congregation where Christians are gathered together—it is significant that the church is called the body of Christ—this phrase seems to imply that the congregation of believers is where Christ is to be found.
- In the bread and wine themselves in some way
- When the bread and wine are consumed by members of the congregation

The question of where Jesus is to be found in a service of Holy Communion is related to the question of what consecration is. There are five main ways of thinking about this question:

- *Transubstantiation:* This is the official teaching of the Roman Catholic Church and is a view held by many others in Western churches. It was officially set out at the Fourth Lateran Council of 1215 referred to above. The idea is that the bread and the wine change their nature so that they become the body and blood of Jesus in something like a literal sense. If they were subjected to chemical analysis they would still be found to be bread and wine but the reality of what they are goes deeper than what a chemical analysis could tell you. This view uses some philosophical terms, chiefly the ideas of substance and accidents. To understand this we need to invoke the idea of ontology. This is the way of talking about what something is in and of itself, that is to say what is its deep and essential nature. The ontology of a chair is what makes it a chair and not a table. You could say that the essence of being a chair is that you can sit on it but it is possible to sit on a table and so when we try to pin down the ontology of a chair we have to find some way of talking about it which describes what it is that is unique in a chair. The substance of something is about its ontology—what it is really—whereas the accident is about what it looks like—that is to say its properties.

This way of thinking about Communion goes back to Ambrose of Milan but the first major discussion of it was triggered by Paschasius Radbertus in the ninth century. He wrote that the bread and wine literally become the body and blood of Jesus because what Jesus said at the Last Supper was 'This is my body/blood' and since God is truth itself this must be taken at face value. He was opposed by Ratramnus who argued that these words of Jesus at the Last Supper are to be taken as metaphorical. After the Fourth Lateran Council, this way of thinking of the bread and wine at Holy Communion, that the substance is changed by God into the body and blood of Jesus while the accidents remain as bread and wine, became widespread beliefs and were imposed as the official teaching of the Roman Catholic Church.

Edward Schillebeeckx thought that most medieval Christians did not believe in a literal change of the bread and wine but opted for the metaphorical approach. This seems quite hard to accept since the literal interpretation is found in Thomas Aquinas and is what the Reformers reacted against. This way of thinking about Holy Communion is also sometimes referred to as the doctrine of the real presence of Christ at the eucharist. However, as we will see, it is possible to believe in Jesus being present (even in a special way) at Holy Communion without taking the literalistic approach to the words of Jesus at the Last Supper.

- *Consubstantiation:* The sixteenth century reformer Martin Luther rejected transubstantiation but wanted to retain the idea that Jesus is specially present in communion, including being specially present in the bread and wine themselves. He therefore talked about Jesus being present 'in, with, through and under' the bread and wine, which is a doctrine known as consubstantiation.
- *Transignification:* This is the view which Schillebeeckx himself opts for. Rather than the substance of the bread and wine being changed at Communion, their significance is changed and this is a change

that cannot be reversed. This can be understood by thinking of a wedding ring. It remains just a band of metal and has a monetary value but when it has been set aside for use as a wedding ring it takes on a significance for the couple concerned as well as for others which cannot be undone and far outweighs its actual monetary value.

- *Memorialism:* For some Christians, Jesus is not present at Holy Communion in any way which is different from how he is present in any other context. What we are doing at Holy Communion is remembering what Jesus did. Some people who take this view even describe Holy Communion as a visual aid given to us by Jesus to remember his death on the cross and what it achieved. In history, this kind of approach is often associated with the Reformer Huldrych Zwingli.
- *Faithful Reception:* Thomas Cranmer came to believe that we encounter Christ when we actually receive the bread and the wine. Christ is present in the receiving. This is Cranmer's reason for opposing the late medieval view that is associated with transubstantiation where you can find Christ in the consecrated elements simply by gazing on them and adoring them.

The practical outworking of Cranmer's view is that it is important that people actually receive the bread and the wine at a service and this is linked with Cranmer's great desire that people should receive both bread and wine, though where this is not possible Christ is received in one or the other. Hence the label that this view is that those who receive the bread and wine faithfully receive Christ.

Remembering

At the Last Supper Jesus said, 'Do this in remembrance of me…' One question which Christians have debated ever since is what exactly we are to do in order to remember Jesus. Another question is what remembering actually means in this context. The Greek word which Paul uses here in his account of the Last Supper is the word *anamnesis*. This Greek word is used in the Greek translation of the Old Testament to translate the Hebrew word *zakar*. There is a considerable amount of agreement that these words go beyond a meaning such as recollection. In English, we can talk about remembering where we have put our car keys or remembering where we first met someone and this is about calling something to mind by retrieving a piece of information. However, we can also use the word 'remember' to imply something a bit more subtle as in something like reliving the moment. This might be what we do when we remember a holiday or a pleasant (or unpleasant!) experience. What the words *anamnesis* and *zakar* imply, then, is that remembering at the eucharist is about inhabiting these events and making them real for us today even if we were personally not there in the first place. This becomes controversial when people want to extend this approach to talk about Jesus being really present at the eucharist—so we are back to questions discussed above. There is also in some Western Catholic theology a sense that the death of Jesus is repeated every time we celebrate Holy Communion. To be fair to those who take this view, they do not think that this denies the uniqueness of the death of Jesus nor that Jesus dies more than once. We do not have to go this far. If we agree that remembering is more than just calling to mind, then at Holy Communion God is making the death of Jesus and its effects real for us once again. As someone once said, when we walk down the aisle to receive communion it is not simply a trip down memory lane.

1 Corinthians 11.23–26 links the Last Supper, celebrating Holy Communion, salvation brought through the death of Jesus and remembering all together:

> 23 For I received from the Lord what I also handed on to you, that the
> Lord Jesus on the night when he was betrayed took a loaf of bread,
> 24 and when he had given thanks, he broke it and said, 'This is my body
> that is for you. Do this in remembrance of me.' 25 In the same way he
> took the cup also, after supper, saying, 'This cup is the new covenant
> in my blood. Do this, as often as you drink it, in remembrance of me.'
> 26 For as often as you eat this bread and drink the cup, you proclaim
> the Lord's death until he comes. (NRSV)

We might note the following points about this passage:

- Giving thanks in v 24 is the word *eucharistein* from which we get the word eucharist.
- There seems to be a play on words in v 23 between the reference to what Paul handed on to the Corinthians and Jesus being betrayed (handed over) since the same Greek word is used in both places.
- The NRSV accurately translates v 24 as 'This is my body that is for you'—there is no word for 'given' in the original.
- Verse 25 introduces the idea that the blood (and presumably also the body) of Jesus is integral to the new covenant which Jesus brings.
- Verse 26 is notable for having past, present and future held together around all of this. In the present, we are eating the bread and drinking the cup and taking part in an act of proclamation. How-

ever, what we are proclaiming is the Lord's death which of course involves us in looking back to the past. We do this while awaiting the return of the Lord in the future so we are looking forwards as well as looking back.

These considerations mean that the question of what we are remembering is not quite as straightforward as it first appears.

- We might simply remember the death of Jesus which is certainly what is in view in the accounts of the Last Supper in the gospels and in 1 Corinthians.
- We might be remembering the suffering, death, ascension and second coming of Jesus. As implied above, you can remember something that is yet to happen if you think of remembering as making something real in the present, whether that event is in the past or future.
- Some people think we should be remembering even more than this by including here the life and teaching of Jesus, in other words remembering the whole of Jesus' ministry, not simply the events at the end of his earthly life.[13]
- The preface to the eucharistic prayer usually involves remembering before God other things such as some of God's mighty acts in salvation. This means that the idea of remembering is already broader in eucharistic prayers than simply remembering the death of Jesus. However, when we come to the part of the prayer known as the anamnesis, we are focusing especially on Jesus and what he has done—so an emphasis on his death and resurrection is central here.

Praying for the Spirit

We noted above that there are two sorts of epiclesis. The consecration epiclesis prays for the Spirit to do something to the bread and wine so they are transformed, whereas the communion epiclesis prays for the Spirit to work through the bread and wine so that those who eat and drink them are transformed. In some of the oldest eucharistic prayers which we have there is also a sense of the Spirit then working through those who have received communion to change the world. The debate that some Christians have had about whether it is right to pray for God to send the Spirit to transform the bread and wine can be seen in a different way if we ask where the activity of the Spirit terminates. If this activity terminates with the congregation or in the world then that sees the transformation of the bread and wine as a means to an end rather than an end in itself. There is a danger that this makes Holy Communion something functional that we do in order to achieve something else but we can avoid this rather limited view of communion and still see that the transformation of the use of the bread and wine leads to transformation elsewhere.

When we (that is, the committee on which I served which produced the CW Eucharistic Prayers) produced the Eucharistic Prayers which are in *Common Worship*, we did not explore the idea of an epiclesis where the activity of the Spirit terminates in the world outside the church, though Eucharistic Prayer F goes a little way in that direction with its response 'Amen. Come Holy Spirit' in the last section of the prayer. The MWB does not go much beyond a communion epiclesis. An epiclesis which sees the action of the Spirit terminating in the world might be called a mission epiclesis. Here is an example of what such an epiclesis might look like:

> May we who eat this bread and drink this wine be transformed by your Spirit to seek your kingdom in the world.

Offering and Sacrifice

There is a consistent biblical theme of offering. There are three ways in which this is discussed.

- Human beings offer themselves and their lives in dedication to God as a response to what God has done, which offering of our lives is described as being a sacrifice.
- Human beings offer worship as a sacrifice to God.
- There is also a well-trodden theological path which sees the death of Jesus as a sacrificial offering, though this is by no means the only way to understand the death of Jesus and does raise some theological issues.

Hosea 14.2 is but one text that refers to praise as an offering: 'We will offer the fruit of our lips' (NRSV). (Though the Hebrew says 'bulls' not 'fruit'—the sense is the same.) A text which is often quoted or alluded to in early Christian writing is Mal 1.10–11: 'I have no pleasure in you, says the Lord of hosts, and I will not accept an offering from your hands. For from the rising of the sun to its setting my name is great among the nations, and in every place incense is offered to my name, and a pure offering; for my name is great among the nations, says the Lord of hosts' (NRSV). What is happening here is that the lives of the people are not in accordance with what God requires and so their worship is not acceptable to him—hence he will not accept their offering. However, God says that he is worshipped in every place and amongst all peoples. In both the negative and positive parts of this quotation, worship is described as an offering.

Psalm 116.17 refers to offering a thanksgiving sacrifice and of course there was an extensive sacrificial system in the Old Testament through which people could worship God by offering sacrifices. Hebrews 13.15 says much the same thing: 'Through him, then, let us continually offer a sacrifice of praise to God, that is, the fruit of lips that confess his name' (NRSV).

There is a frequent theme in the Old Testament prophets which links worship with the way in which people live their lives. It is no good offering worship to God in the hope that he will accept it, if you are not living a life which pleases God. This will involve social justice within your community. Perhaps the clearest expression of this is in Amos 5:

> **21** I hate and I reject your big celebrations,
> and I take no delight in your gatherings.[14]
> **22** Even though you offer me your burnt-offerings and grain-offerings,
> I will not accept them;
> and the offerings of well-being of your fatted animals—
> I won't pay any attention to them.
> **23** Take away from me the noise of your songs;
> and as to the sound of your harps—I won't listen to them.
> **24** But let justice flow down like waters,
> and righteousness like an ever-flowing stream.

I like this passage because God rejects all types of worship. Charismatics are out of favour (v 23) and so are those who like to observe all the festivals and saints' days of the Christian year (v 21). Sacramental worship fares no better (v 22).

Romans 12.1 refers to worship being expressed as the sacrifice of our lives in dedication to God: 'I appeal to you therefore, brothers and sisters, by the mercies of God, to present your bodies as a living sacrifice, holy and acceptable to God, which is your spiritual worship.' This picks up the Old Testament theme of the authenticity of worship being tested by how you live your life.

Hebrews 10.10–18 is perhaps the clearest expression in the New Testament of the idea that Jesus offers himself as a sacrifice and that no other sacrifice or offering is required in order to gain salvation. In vv 12–14 we read, 'But when Christ had offered for all time a single sacrifice for sins, "he sat down at the right hand of God"...For by a single offering he has perfected for all time those who are sanctified…' Christian teaching has seen the offering of our lives as being a response to what Jesus has done for us rather than a means of winning salvation.

This then gives us the theological framework in which we can understand the idea of sacrifice. God in Christ makes the sacrifice on the cross which brings salvation to us. We respond to what God in Christ has done by offering our lives and our worship in a sacrificial way—that is to say by offering them in total devotion.

The New Testament does not talk about Holy Communion as a sacrifice but by the third century this way of speaking of the eucharist was beginning to appear. Writing in the second century after Jesus, Justin Martyr refers to Christian prayer as sacrifice but also links the eucharist and offering: '[God] then speaks of those gentiles, namely us, who in every place offer sacrifices to him, *ie* the bread of the eucharist, and also the cup of the eucharist.'[15] Church leaders often spoke of the offering / sacrifice of praise but it is Cyprian, Bishop of Carthage (between 249 and 258), who first takes the step of describing the eucharist as a sacrifice and the presiding minister as a priest offering the sacrifice.[16]

It is not difficult to see how this happened. If worship can be seen as our sacrificial response to the sacrifice made by Jesus and if Holy Communion is the supreme act of worship, then it is quite logical to talk about Communion as a sacrifice. However, it is easy to let the framework I have been sketching out here become out of focus and to begin to think that when we offer the sacrifice of worship, that somehow is effective in saving us. As I have been pointing out, it is in fact a *response* to the death of Jesus, which death is the means of salvation, rather than the worship we offer being the means of salvation itself.

The approach which saw the eucharist as a sacrifice offered to God grew throughout the Middle Ages until it became the standard way of thinking of the eucharist in the Western church. This is what the Protestant reformers reacted against and rejected, as it undermined the once for all nature of Jesus' death as sacrifice. The Church of England and the British Methodist Church have avoided using such language in their eucharistic prayers. An attempt to introduce the phrase 'We offer this bread and this cup' into a Church of England eucharistic prayer in 1966 (when the production of new liturgies was beginning) was rejected.

Thanksgiving

If the eucharistic prayer did evolve out of Jesus giving thanks for the food at the Last Supper, it is not difficult to see how the theme of thanksgiving is central to the eucharistic prayer. The very title gives us the clue since the word 'eucharist' means thanksgiving. In terms of the structure of a eucharistic prayer, the preface is all about thanksgiving. We give thanks to God for what God has done and we can mention different things in different eucharistic prayers as well as having seasonal and topical thanksgivings in this part of the prayer. This leads up to giving praise to God in the Sanctus and also then focusing on giving thanks to God for what he has done for us in Jesus when we come to the next part of the eucharistic prayer, focused on the institution narrative.

It is rather sad that the way many ministers pray the eucharistic prayer gives no clue that this is meant to be a tremendous prayer of thanksgiving. The style and tone are often downbeat and sometimes any music that is used to sing items such as the Sanctus is not such as actually encourages praise. Careful thought must be given to these practical matters.

It is possible to weave into the eucharistic prayer an opportunity for members of the congregation to give thanks for things, though this requires a skilful minister presiding and also probably a relatively small congregation in the building where people can hear each other![17]

5 Praying with Understanding

In this booklet, the emphasis has been on understanding what is happening in a eucharistic prayer so I have focused on structure and theology. However, this is rather like understanding how a car engine works without ever going for a drive. The whole point of a eucharistic prayer is that it should be prayed and should lead to us receiving communion (and deepening our relationship with God).

There are a whole lot of other issues around eucharistic prayers to do with how they deepen our spirituality and how they are to be staged and performed. (You may not like those last two terms but the practical aspects of how our worship is carried out are very important and to talk about staging and performance does not mean being false or mechanistic—it just means paying attention to the practical aspects.) The Group for the Renewal of Worship which produces this series of Grove booklets hopes to produce a companion booklet to this one which looks at the spirituality of eucharistic prayers and also deals with some of the practical aspects of praying them.[18]

However, it is important to pray with understanding so that what I have discussed in this booklet is not disconnected from the life of prayer or indeed the life of discipleship, but it is an important part of it. Understanding how a eucharistic prayer works and what it is trying to do will help us to pray it as a genuine prayer. It is indeed a rather more complicated prayer than many of those we use. It is also probably more formal and longer. For all these reasons, it is important that we understand it so that it becomes *our* prayer and not just a text which we are instructed to use. If we are in a position to write our own eucharistic prayer (as Methodists are but Anglicans are not), we will need to understand what this involves.[19]

Notes

1 P F Bradshaw and M E Johnson (eds), *Prayer of the Eucharist Early and Reformed, Alcuin Club Collections* 94 (Collegeville, MN: Liturgical Press, 2019 (fourth edition)), revising the book of the same title by R D C Jasper and G J Cuming from 1975.

2 The most up to date approach (but a complex read) is in P F Bradshaw and M E Johnson, *The Eucharistic Liturgies: Their Evolution and Interpretation, Alcuin Club Collections* 87 (London: SPCK, 2012).

3 See, for example, G Lathrop, *Holy Things* (Minneapolis, MN: Fortress Press, 1993)—especially section 2.

4 The report can be found at https://www.oikoumene.org/resources/documents/ditchingham-report-faith-and-order and the quotation is from section 4.

5 First published in 1945 by the Dacre Press but republished a number of times and still available.

6 And their successors the MWB and CW continue this.

7 See Richard Buxton in K Stevenson (ed), *Liturgy Reshaped* (London: SPCK, 1982) ch 6

8 See A Atherstone and A Goddard, *'Drink This, All of You'* (Grove Worship booklet W250).

9 See C Buchanan, *Eucharistic Consecration in Common Worship* (Grove Worship booklet W213).

10 That is the bread and wine become the body and blood of Christ—see discussion below.

11 G Cuming, *He Gave Thanks: An Introduction to the Eucharistic Prayer* (Grove Liturgical Studies 28) p 18.

12 M Carothers, *Power in Praise* (Eastbourne: Kingsway, 1974).

13 Jim Farwell of Virginia Theological Seminary has argued this: https://www.youtube.com/watch?v=nCWpb5QukdE

14 Literally 'I do not smell your assemblies for worship' so perhaps we might translate 'I don't like the smell of it!'

15 Justin Dialogue with Trypho 41, available at http://www.earlychristianwritings.com/text/justinmartyr-dialoguetrypho.html

16 Richard Hanson describes this evolution in detail, referring to a number of early Christian writers, in *Eucharistic Offering in the Early Church* (Grove Liturgical Studies 19).

17 See C Read, *How to Preside at Holy Communion* (Grove Worship booklet W214) for practical advice on this.

18 Though I have addressed some of the practical aspects in *How to Preside at Holy Communion*—see note 19.

19 Though in the Church of England you can write your own proper prefaces.

20 See also *New Patterns for Worship* section G Notes.

21 See MWB pp 221f.